Transforming Anger to

Personal Power

An Anger Management
Curriculum for Grades 6-12

D1520116

Susan Gingras Fitzell

Research Press
2612 North Mattis Avenue
Champaign, Illinois 61822
(800) 519-2707
www.researchpress.com

Composition by Jeff Helgesen
Cover design by Linda Brown, Positive I.D. Graphic Design, Inc.
Printed by Malloy, Inc.

ISBN-13: 978-0-87822-538-5
ISBN-10: 0-87822-538-2
Library of Congress Control Number 2006939309

To Mike Torch, Jean Rinker, Abby Osman, and Jeffery Sullivan, for the encouragement and opportunities that made this book possible

A special thank-you to Arlene Iverson, for her help in editing and clarifying the objectives

Contents

Handouts

Anger Management: One Tool in Peace Education

For the eighth time in eight weeks, I walked into the small room and sat in the circle of chairs. Seven sets of eyes watched me, a myriad of expressions on their faces. The faces have changed since week one, from looks that expressed apathy, anger, and dismay at being forced into this circle to receptiveness, acceptance, and comfort with the group.

I looked at my co-facilitator and then around the room at the students and posed the question "What is one thing that you have learned about anger in the past seven weeks?" Eyes watched me. I learned early on that I could not pose a question to this group and expect a response unless I called on them, one by one, encouraging participation. Once they started talking, however, the floodgates often opened, moving the group from passive observers to active contributors.

I looked at Matt and waited. I knew I could count on him to get the ball rolling. He didn't disappoint me. "Anger is a secondary emotion," he answered. "What does that mean?" I replied. "It means that there's other feelings inside that come first, but those feelings turn to anger, and it happens so fast!" he said. I smiled and thanked him, then looked to the young woman sitting next to him.

Sophisticated and reserved, she might appear to be an unlikely candidate for this group. Appearances mean nothing. A fly on the wall would see little commonality among these participants—they represent a cross-section of peer groups. Students are referred to the program by an administrator or a counselor, or they are self-referred. There's a waiting list.

1

The administration presents this group as an alternative to out-of-school suspension. If students choose participation in this eight-week anger management group, their suspension is waived. If students miss sessions, they must serve the suspension. Overall, this approach works and keeps attendance consistent.

Ellen looked at me thoughtfully. She answered that she had learned that people had choices when they felt angry. People could choose to walk away or change the way they think about a situation. Using the opening she presented, I reviewed the physiological and psychological aspects of anger and the anger reaction that we had talked about a few weeks earlier.

"Anger is triggered," I said. "The body goes into a fight or flight response, and then self-talk happens. If you choose positive self-talk, you will be able to choose your action and take positive steps to deal with your anger. If you choose negative self-talk, anger will escalate." I framed what Ellen contributed in words we used during the lessons. Framing concepts with language that helps people to feel they can choose their behavior and control their anger is key to success in any anger management program.

Ed spoke out, "Well, if some jerk hits on my girlfriend, it makes me mad." I looked around the room, seeing the light go on in their eyes. They knew what was coming. Mike, my co-facilitator asked, "Can someone 'make' you mad?" "No," several answered, however reluctantly. The consensus was that anger is triggered.

I asked, "Why is that so important to understand?" They took stabs at what I'm looking for, but no one hit on the point I wanted to reiterate and stress. "If someone 'makes' you mad, who has control over your emotions? What does that language tell you about who is in control?" Steve, usually passive and quietly resistant, answered, "The other person has control."

"If something triggers your anger, who has control? Who has the power?" I could see the light dawn in their eyes as I looked around the room. "We do," they answered.

The goal of this anger management program is to help kids to see that they are not helpless victims of society. They have an opportunity to take control of their lives and emotions and choose healthier responses to anger. Understanding the social, cultural, and personal influences that shape their thinking, using empowering language, and owning their behavior are key to the effectiveness of the group sessions.

My co-facilitator and I have seen the effect of the program on students' behavior in the halls, in the administrative office, and in private sessions. Students have a new frame of reference with which to view their thinking and behavior. They catch themselves in the process of making a choice— something clicks, and they make a better choice. When we talk with them outside of sessions, as role models and guides, we have language we can use that they understand.

I knew we were making a difference when one student, with a twinkle in his eyes, asked me, "How are you feeling?" Knowing what he was looking for, I answered, "Mad!" He said, "Mad is a secondary emotion. You can't use that word. What are you really feeling?"

Anger management is a critical component in any peace education curriculum because when anger is mismanaged, it is a major obstacle to peace. Before we can consider making inroads to world peace, we need to start with what's happening at home with our youth and in our hearts. For the teens I work with, that means learning to deal with their anger constructively.

Introduction

This book is the result of five years of working with middle school and high school students in an evolving anger management program. What you see here today is not what I started with and most likely will change as I learn more about what works and what doesn't.

One thing you won't see in this program is a multitude of worksheets. I know that I'm taking a risk in not including worksheets because teachers, counselors, and program facilitators generally like them. In my experience, however, students generally do not. I tried a student handbook. It didn't work. I found it on the floor and under the desks. Worksheets were filled out with halfhearted effort, and there was much grumbling about being made to write! Some students could not write very well at all, and that was part of the problem. Although the program includes handouts, there is only one worksheet in this program, and it is an essential exercise. I explain it as such to the students, and they get over their complaints about writing pretty quickly.

I have found that adolescents want to talk, think, share, compare, evaluate, analyze, and challenge. That's the work that needs to be done. It's their work. So, consequently, I threw out the student handbook and all the worksheets. Instead, I have tried to format the lessons so that the information is clear and easy for facilitators and students to follow.

Here are the most important aspects of this book.

The progression

One lesson builds from another, and I strongly suggest following the existing order of lessons.

The philosophy

This book is about teaching students to keep their power. It's not about adults trying to fix youth, tell them how to live, or show them that adults know better. This philosophy is important because adolescents will tune out if they believe that the adults in the room want to change them to fit an adult agenda.

The format

These lessons can be taught as classroom lessons by teachers. However, as an anger management curriculum used in a psychoeducational group, it is best run by co-facilitators, preferably a male and a female. One of the two ideally would be a counselor. The other might be an educational consultant or psychoeducator, social worker, or other professional knowledgeable about youth.

The focus

The group sessions are intended to be used for psychoeducational purposes and not as therapy. If this program is used as a therapy program, it is used outside the scope of the curriculum and consequently may not be successful.

The follow-up

The lessons in and of themselves are not enough. Students must know that they have a place to go or a person to talk to when they are in need. Often, a student will want to discuss something personal in the group. Individual issues should be avoided. This is not a therapy group. If a lesson isn't taught because the group becomes more therapeutic instead, it undermines the effectiveness of the program.

The research model

The program draws from several bodies of knowledge: martial arts and Eastern philosophy, cognitive intervention techniques, brain research theories, and educational psychology.

ᘒᘇᘒᘆᘉ

An important part of the program is the visual representation of the ideas conveyed in the lessons. Appendix A includes a number of sample charts that teachers and other program leaders may use when conducting the lessons.

The most effective way to use the samples is to create your own version of them on the pages of a flip chart, adapting them to fit your own circumstances and group. The illustrations on the sample charts are purposely simple to make reproducing them easy, even for those who are not artistically inclined.

It is also possible to use the sample charts to create overhead transparencies or to provide students with copies of the charts as handouts as the lessons proceed. However, these methods will not allow you to reveal information a bit at a time in the way using a flip chart will. Revealing content as the lesson progresses creates anticipation and can help students stay engaged with the lesson.

When appropriate, lessons include instructions to present particular charts. When these instructions appear, you may display the complete chart or give the information gradually, whichever you choose. When instructions to present a chart appear, the content of the chart appears in the lesson for reference.

This curriculum is a beginning, a place to start the change process. Students have taken years to learn their present ways of managing anger. It may take years for them to learn new ways. This curriculum is a solid start.

Anger Management: An Opportunity

Key Concepts

◆ Enforced ground rules are essential for the success of the program and the safety of all students involved.

◆ Students have a choice: To accept an opportunity or to reject it.

◆ The program is an educational program, not a counseling or therapeutic program.

Materials

Anger Management: An Opportunity (Chart 1.1)

Procedure

1. Present Chart 1.1.

   Anger Management: An Opportunity

   Ground rules

   Why are you here?

   You have a choice: Open mind or closed mind.

   Expectations

Ground Rules

2. Tell students:

   ◆ In order for everyone to feel safe, ground rules are necessary.

3. Ask students:

   ◆ What ground rules do you think the group should establish?

4. Brainstorm:

   ◆ Possible ground rules.

5. Decide on rules for the group.

   Examples

   ◆ Respect others in the group.

     (Define what this means to the group. For instance, one person talks at a time, good listening, no putdowns, etc.)

   ◆ No verbal or physical violence or threats of violence.

   ◆ We may not use the names of people who are not here to defend themselves.

   ◆ No disclosing of what others in the group have done.

   ◆ What happens in here stays in here.

Why Are You Here?

1. Tell students firmly:

   ◆ Today will be your one opportunity to ask questions or vent about why you are here. After today, that kind of discussion will not be allowed.

   ◆ This rule is necessary because if we spend time every session rehashing this issue, we will not get through the curriculum, and consequently it will be a waste of your time and ours.

   ◆ Our hope is that you will use the group as an opportunity to grow and learn ways to get more of what YOU want out of life.

   NOTE: Use this first session to allow students to vent about why they are in the anger management program, to ask questions, and to discuss concerns. Permission to vent and express feelings about being in the program during this session diminishes the need and possibility of future sessions' being derailed or sidetracked by students' need to vent.

2. Ask students questions to open up discussion.

   Examples

   ◆ Why are you here?

   ◆ Do you feel you belong here?

   ◆ What happened that caused you to be in this group?

◆ How do you feel about being here?

◆ Do you believe this group can help you? Why or why not?

You Have a Choice: Open Mind or Closed Mind

1. Discuss:

   ◆ You have a choice—to have an open mind or a closed mind.

   NOTE: At the high school level many, if not most, students resent being sent to an anger management program. They come in angry, resentful, and without any buy-in. It is important to plant seeds to get them to see that this is an opportunity for them, not a punishment.

2. Set the stage by saying:

   ◆ We (co-facilitators) are not here to turn you into somebody else. We are not here to tell you that you are wrong or bad. We are not here to try to "fix" you. Rather, we are here to help you stick up for yourself in a way that works for you. We are here to teach you options for your anger, so that when you do get angry, the choices you make will benefit you in the end.

   ◆ We are not here to benefit the teachers, the school, or anyone else. We care that you are making choices that give you what you want in the end: success, staying out of trouble, not being anyone's victim or puppet. We are here for you.

   NOTE: You can be as specific as you'd like in this statement. Also, although the first day is not necessarily the right time to introduce key phrases and metaphors, you might use the following phrases and metaphors to plant seeds of change as you work through these lessons. Where appropriate, teach and remind students of main concepts, using thought-provoking questions and statements:

   What is your self-talk? When you say _____ , what are you thinking? If you were a private investigator hired to determine what thoughts were guiding your actions, what would you find?

   When someone triggers your anger and you react, you are like a puppet on a string, moving powerlessly according to the moves of another person. Do you want to be someone else's puppet?

   Some adolescents may not like to imagine themselves as being someone else's puppet. Another analogy is a fish taking bait from a hook.

Expectations

1. Discuss expectations, both yours and the students'. Tell students:

   ◆ This is not a therapy group. What we do here is educate. However, if you need to talk one-on-one about your concerns, things that happen that anger you personally, something that happens in the hall or the classroom, please make an appointment to come back and see us so that we can talk and you can get the time that you need.

   NOTE: Differentiating between a therapy group and a psychoeducational group is very important. Many of the students will have participated in therapy groups and will want to proceed as if this is another one. For these lessons to work, the instructional material must be taught. If sessions are spent discussing one student's recent crisis, the group becomes a therapy group rather than an anger management program based on a curriculum. If the group focuses on students' individual issues, it will be difficult to finish the program.

2. Answer any questions students may have.

LESSON 2 BACKGROUND
Our Feelings Are Valid

This lesson introduces the concept of primary and secondary emotions, among other ideas. A primary emotion is what we feel first. For example, fear, anger, joy, sadness, and acceptance are considered primary emotions. A secondary emotion is what evolves from the primary emotion after cognition. For example, a prankster startles me, and I feel fear instantly. I "think" it was deliberate, so then I feel anger toward the prankster. Although anger is labeled a primary emotion by some theorists, it is also often considered a secondary emotion by others.

Primary emotions such as fear or sadness, when intense enough, can lead to anger. In addition, we might feel insulted, pressured, cheated, or the like. If these feelings are at a low level, we are not likely to say we feel angry. However, if they are intense, we commonly say we feel angry. Anger came after the first feelings intensified.

Depression is another example of a secondary emotion. Depression can include feeling discouraged, hopeless, lonely, isolated, misunderstood, overwhelmed, attacked, invalidated, unsupported, and so on. Normally, depression includes a combination of feelings.

"Catch-all" statements such as "I'm angry" or "I'm depressed" do not help us much when it comes to identifying our unmet emotional needs. When all I can say is "I feel angry," neither I nor anyone else knows what would help me to feel better. However, if I say I feel pressured, trapped, or disrespected, it is much clearer what my unmet emotional need is and what would help me to feel better. A simple but effective technique, then, is to identify the primary emotion underlying the anger. Therefore, for the purpose of this lesson, anger is considered a secondary emotion. The feelings that lead up to anger are considered primary emotions because they come first.

Resources

Elder, John. (2004)."The Anger Management Pyramid," Retrieved June 1, 2006 from http://www.jelder.com

Munro, Kali. (2002). "Feelings: Identifying How You Feel," *Resources for Healing.* Retrieved June 1, 2006, from http://www.kalimunro.com/article_feelings_body.html

Straker, David. (2002–2006). *Changing Minds,* Retrieved June 1, 2006, from http://changingminds.org/explanations/emotions/basic%20emotions.htm

LESSON 2

Our Feelings Are Valid

Key Concepts

- Adolescents have a right to their feelings.
- Human emotions are valid.
- We are responsible for our feelings and actions.
- There are two types of emotion: primary and secondary.
- Anger can be defined.

Materials

Are the Following Statements True? (Chart 2.1)

Name Some Primary Emotions (Chart 2.2)

We Own Our Feelings (Chart 2.3)

We Have a Choice (Chart 2.4)

When We Feel Angry . . . (Chart 2.5)

Copies of the MOODZ handout (optional; Chart 6.1, on page 109)

Procedure

Are the Following Statements True?

1. Present Chart 2.1.

   Are the Following Statements True?

   I have the *right* to feel what I feel.

   My feelings are valid.

   I am fully *responsible* for my feelings; I own what I feel.

2. Ask students:

   - Are these statements true?
   - Do you have the right to feel what you feel?

- Do you believe that you should be allowed to express your feelings?
- Have people ever told you, "You shouldn't feel that way?"
- Have people ever said, "You are overreacting!"
- How did it feel when people said these things? What message did it give you?

3. Consider asking more probing questions if emotions that often escalate to anger don't come up. For example:

Has anyone ever experienced too much homework due all the same day? How did that feel?

Has you ever failed a test that you studied for? How did that feel?

Has anyone ever been told, "You think you're all that!" or "You're stupid"?

Ask questions that are likely to elicit the words *frustration, overwhelmed, jealous, disappointed, disrespected,* and so on.

4. Discuss:
- How it feels when people dismiss our feelings.

5. Tell students:
- You have the right to feel what you feel. Your feelings are valid.
- Not only do you have the right to feel, you are also fully responsible for those feelings and what you do about them.

Name Some Primary Emotions

1. Present Chart 2.2.

   Name Some Primary Emotions

   ANGER is a secondary emotion.

2. Discuss:
- The difference between primary and secondary emotions.

ACTIVITY: NAME SOME PRIMARY EMOTIONS

- Ask students: What are some primary emotions?
- List the emotion words students name on Chart 2.2.
- Students can refer to the MOODZ handout if you wish.

NOTE: Be sure that the words you list in the activity are emotions and not actions. Students often have difficulty coming up with emotion language. For example, they will say, "I feel like I want to beat him up!" or "I feel like I want to tell her off!" (Those are actions, not feelings.) They need to learn to say, "I feel hurt" or "I feel disrespected."

We Own Our Feelings

1. Present Chart 2.3.

    ### We Own Our Feelings

    Responsibility = Ownership

    No one can put feelings inside of us.

    No one can *MAKE* us angry.

    People *TRIGGER* our anger.

    We *CHOOSE* how we feel.

2. Discuss:

    ◆ The concept that no one can MAKE us feel anything.

    ◆ As an example, ask, "Can I make you feel happy about being here? Failing a test? Visiting a relative that you dislike?" *(Students usually respond no.)*

    ◆ Say, "If I can't make you happy, I can't make you angry, and I can't MAKE you feel what you don't want or choose to feel."

We Have a Choice

1. Present Chart 2.4

    ### We Have a Choice

    Accept your feelings

    AND

    Choose your actions wisely.

2. Discuss:

    ◆ Students' reactions to the idea of "choosing" how you feel.

    ◆ Reinforce the concept that in choosing, we are empowered. When we don't choose, we are reacting like a puppet on a string and giving away our power.

NOTE: You might also use the analogy of a baited hook and a fish. The baited hook correlates to the name-calling, button pushing, and banter that often provokes conflict and anger. The fish correlates to the student, who makes a choice to take the bait or refuse to take it.

An excellent resource on this topic is *Simon's Hook: A Story about Teases and Put-Downs,* by Karen Gedig Burnett, with illustrations by Laurie Barrows. (See the recommended resources at the end of this book.) It is a picture book; however, if you can present it to the students in a way that they don't feel like they are being talked down to, it can be quite effective. One possible way to do this is to ask them if this story would help teach the concept to younger children.

When We Feel Angry

1. Read and discuss statements from Chart 2.5.

   When We Feel Angry . . .

   We are not BAD . . . we are angry.

   What we do with that anger is a choice we make.

   If we make a mistake, we are not bad . . . we are learning.

2. Tell students:

   ◆ In our society, there is a tendency to feel victimized when things don't go the way that we want. Prisons are full of people who would tell you that they are victims of an unfair system or that they were mistreated as children.

   ◆ When we take responsibility for our behavior and our choices, we are no longer victims. We gain the power to choose.

   ◆ When we own what happens to us and make choices about those things, we are able to achieve control over ourselves and, to some degree, our environment. We cannot change or improve what we don't control. Taking control of our behavior gives us the power to avoid being a victim.

   Closing thought: Making a conscious choice is always better than blindly reacting.

LESSON 3 BACKGROUND
Understanding Anger and Its Triggers

Neuroscientists recently discovered a brain pathway that acts as a super-sonic express route to the brain's emotional centers.[1] This neural back alley (which appears to be reserved for emotional emergencies) bypasses the neocortex entirely, routing information from the thalamus directly to the "amygdala," a tiny structure in the limbic system that has been identified as the brain's emotional alarm center. The amygdala scans the information for potential danger: "Is this bad? Could it hurt me?"

Neuroscientists believe that in most instances, the amygdala makes its snap judgments based on being the repository of emotional memory. Stress seems to increase the functioning of the amygdala, kicking it into overdrive, thereby facilitating extremely potent learned fear. If the information registers as dangerous, the amygdala broadcasts a distress signal to the entire brain, which, in turn, triggers a cascade of physiological responses—from a speeded-up heart rate to jacked-up blood pressure to mobilized muscles to release of the "fight or flight" hormones, adrenaline and noradrenaline.

> **Noradrenaline,** also known as norepinephrine (the anger hormone) is secreted by the medulla (inner portion) of the adrenal gland and from the locus coeruleus in the brain stem, which (together with epinephrine) brings about the changes in the body known as the "fight or flight" reaction (or "stress reaction"). Some of the actions of this hormone on various bodily systems include increased metabolism, increased blood pressure, increased mental activity, increased blood flow to the muscles, and increased heart rate. These reactions

---

[1]This paragraph and the next are adapted by permission from "The Emotional Imperative," by B. Atkinson, 1999, *Family Therapy Networker, 23*(4), 22–33.

prepare the individual to deal with perceived threats or stress by enhancing capabilities to fight or to flee.

Adrenaline, also known as epinephrine (the fear hormone) is a secretion of the adrenal glands in times of heightened emotion or stress.

Dopamine. As a chemical messenger, dopamine is similar to adrenaline. Dopamine affects brain processes that control movement, emotional response, and the ability to experience pleasure and pain.

Cortisol. Cortisol is called the stress hormone because its levels rise in the bloodstream following both physical and psychological stressors. Cortisol's functions in the body include regulation of blood pressure and cardiovascular function as well as regulation of the body's use of proteins, carbohydrates, and fats. Cortisol is part of the body's fight-or-flight response. Following a stressful event or an injury, the adrenal glands increase the secretion of cortisol. The hormone raises blood sugar to provide additional fuel, temporarily slows down some essential bodily functions, and helps boost the heart rate so a person can fight off or run away from a threat.

Other important definitions include the following:

Noradrenergic system, also known as **locus coeruleus.** This system involves processes relating to particular nerve cell fibers in the release of neurotransmitters. The locus coeruleus supplies **noradrenaline/ norepinephrine** throughout the central nervous system.

Stimulus/stimuli, trigger is anything causing a response.

Amygdala. Brain. (1) An almond-shaped neurological structure involved in producing and responding to nonverbal signs of anger, avoidance, defensiveness, and fear; (2) A small mass of gray matter that inspires aversive cues, such as the freeze reaction, sweaty palms, and the tense-mouth display; (3) A primeval arousal center, originating in early fish species, which is central to the expression of negative emotions in man.[2]

---

[2]The definition of *amygdala* and the comments on usage and "neuro notes" on page 21 have been adapted by permission from *The Nonverbal Dictionary: 1998–2005,* by D. Givens, Center for Nonverbal Studies. Retrieved June 2, 2006, from http://citationmachine.net/index.php

Usage: Many gestures reflect the amygdala's turmoil. If we are feeling anxious at a meeting, for example, we may unconsciously flex our arms, lean away, or angle away from people who upset us. Lip, neck, and shoulder muscles may tense as the amygdala activates brain stem circuits designed to produce protective facial expressions and protective postures. The amygdala also prompts releases of adrenaline and other hormones into the bloodstream, thus stepping up a flight response and disrupting the control of rational thought.

Neuro notes. In addition to its other duties, the amygdala's gray matter evolved to mediate the evolutionary ancient chemical nervous system, represented today by our bloodstream. Working through the hypothalamus, the amygdala releases excitatory hormones into circulating blood. After surgical removal of the amygdala, growls, screams, angry voices, and other negative signs may lose their meaning and become incomprehensible as afferent cues.

⊙⊱⊰⊙

Learning to identify when you are in a fight or flight state is the first step in decreasing how long and how intensely you remain in the anger reaction. Brain studies suggest that the moment you become self-aware of escalating emotions, you activate the prefrontal lobes, which in turn reduce stress hormones and allow a state of calm to return. Therefore, it's important to try to notice any changes happening in the body, investigate the thoughts feeding the stress, and change the self-talk to be more constructive.

Understanding Anger and Its Triggers

Key Concepts

◆ Physiological changes occur when anger is triggered.

◆ Anger is physiological and normal.

◆ Fight-or-flight responses result when anger is triggered.

◆ Events don't *make* us angry; they *trigger* our anger.

Materials

For this lesson, you will need to prepare a flip chart by writing "What Makes You Angry?" at the top of a blank page (see Chart 3.2a, on page 104). During the lesson, you will change this chart to look like Chart 3.2b.

Physiological Definitions (Chart 3.1)

Anger Reaction! (Chart 3.3)

Procedure

Physiological Definitions

1. Present Chart 3.1.

   Physiological Definitions

   Noradrenaline: Neurotransmitter regulates [heartbeat, breathing, body temperature].

   Adrenaline

   Stimulus/stimuli = trigger

   How does your body feel when you get ANGRY?

2. Discuss each term's role in the anger process.

3. Ask students:

   ◆ How does your body feel when you get angry? *(Students may need prompting to get started.)*

   ◆ What physically happens in your body?

   ◆ How does your stomach feel?

   ◆ How do your hands feel?

   ◆ What do you notice about your legs? Body? Neck?

   ◆ Do you feel anything in the cheeks of your face?

4. Discuss physical reactions to anger.

   ◆ Pull from the group the physical effects anger has on the body by using the preceding questions and adding your own probing questions. Responses may include the following:

   Faster breathing

   Accelerated heartbeat

   Rise in blood pressure

   Clammy hands

   Rigid body

   Jittery legs

   Knotted stomach

   Red face

   "Head rush"

   Tunnel vision

5. Explain the fight-or-flight response:

   ◆ Fight or flight is a reaction that occurs in the body when we are faced with a sudden, unexpected threat or source of stress. The name of this reaction comes from the fact that an animal confronted with danger almost immediately decides to fight or to run.

   ◆ At this time, there is a sudden release of the hormones adrenaline and noradrenaline, triggering increases in heart rate and breathing, constricting blood vessels in many parts of the body, and tightening muscles. Blood supply is increased to organs involved in the fight or flight—the muscles, brain, lungs, and heart.

◆ Through these actions, the body prepares for a confrontation (fight) or a fast escape (flight).

6. How does this response to stress relate to people?

◆ We have the same fight-or-flight mechanism in our bodies. When our brain perceives a threat, it reacts to protect us by preparing our bodies to fight or run.

◆ The brain's reaction does not differentiate between the threat of words (such as name-calling) and the threat of physical danger (such as a tiger charging towards us). It reacts the same way in both situations.

◆ It does not matter that one source of threat or danger is physical and the other is verbal. The threat may even be something as subtle as a dirty look.

7. Tell students:

◆ Your body reacts to anger physically.

◆ Anger is a chain of simultaneous physical and mental reactions. It happens quickly as one of the responses to threat. It takes less than a second to react! It is a normal part of our survival mechanism.

◆ Many of us are completely unaware of the signals our body gives us as we begin to go into a fight-or-flight reaction. We often simply ignore the signs.

◆ The key to beginning to control anger is to recognize those signals in our bodies before it's too late!

◆ Once you have learned to identify the physical signs and behavioral symptoms of your anger, the next step is learning to identify the *triggers* of your anger so that you can decide what to do about the anger you are feeling. Triggers may be different for each of us.

ACTIVITY: NOTICE HOW YOUR BODY REACTS

Encourage students to apply what they have learned:

◆ Between now and the next meeting, be a "reaction detective." Investigate how your body reacts to different stresses in your life, especially anger.

◆ Try to notice when your body starts to react to a situation: Stop and watch. The better you get at noticing how your body is reacting to a situation, the easier it will be to use tools to manage your anger.

What Triggers Your Anger?

1. Present the flip chart you have prepared. (It should look like Chart 3.2a.)

    What Makes You Angry?

2. Ask students:

    ◆ If you don't want to be here, can I *make* you happy about being here? *(Most students will say no.)*

    ◆ Why can't I make you happy if you don't want to be happy?

    ◆ If I want to make you mad, can I do that? *(Most students will say yes.)*

    ◆ Why can I make you mad, but I can't make you happy?

    ◆ Is it possible for me to make you feel anything if you don't want to feel it?

3. Discuss how the language we use causes us to give our power away when we say someone else can make us angry.

    Ask students:

    ◆ Suppose I am happily going about my business, and you come by and call me a name. If I get very upset and start yelling at you, who has the power over my emotions?

    ◆ If you are talking behind my back, and I overhear you and start slumping my shoulders, looking upset, and showing it, who has the power?

    ◆ In both of these situations, when we let someone else cause us to get upset, show we are upset, or react in anger, we give away our power. Like a puppet on a string, we react to their behavior, thereby giving them control over us.

- ◆ Here's the fishing analogy: Suppose the behavior of the other person is bait. If we take the bait, we give away our power. We are hooked on the fishing line. If we choose not to take the bait, we keep our power. We are not hooked.

4. Ask students:

- ◆ Who is in control if someone is "making" me angry?
- ◆ Who is in control if my anger is triggered?

5. Tell students:

- ◆ When you change your language and thinking from "He made me angry" to "That pushed my buttons" or "That triggered my anger," you keep your personal power because you are in control.

- ◆ When you say and think that someone can make you angry, like a puppet on a string (or a fish on a hook), reacting to some else's actions, you give away your power. The other person is in control.

- ◆ When you acknowledge that someone triggered your anger, you own your behavior and, therefore, you are in control.

ACTIVITY: WHAT TRIGGERS YOUR ANGER?

Refer to the question "What Makes You Angry?" on your flip chart.

- ◆ Cross out "Makes You Angry" and add above it "Triggers Your Anger."

    NOTE: Changing the chart in this way makes the change in language concrete, thereby emphasizing the difference between these two concepts.

Ask students: What triggers your anger?

- ◆ Write down student responses on the chart as accurately as you can. If you shorten statements, be sure to summarize first and have the student verify that it is what he or she meant.

- ◆ For example, you might get the response "Stupid people make me angry." Ask the student to clarify who "stupid people" are and what they do that makes them stupid. Often, the responses are very different from one student to the next.

NOTE: It's very important not to impose your thinking on this process. Do not pass judgment on the responses. Simply write them down and ask for clarification where needed.

This is also a great opportunity to start pointing out how different our perceptions are and how we CHOOSE to react differently to those perceptions based on the way we interpret what we see or hear.

Take comments until the chart is full.

Tell students:

◆ These triggers set off a series of physical reactions in our bodies that we will call the *anger reaction*. This happens in approximately two-tenths of a second.

Anger Reaction

1. Present Chart 3.3.

   Anger Reaction!

   Triggering event

   Perceived threat

   Physical reaction

   Negative self-talk

   Primary emotion

   ANGER REACTION

   Hindsight

2. Provide examples of *triggering events* (or draw them from students):
   ◆ Name-calling and putdowns
   ◆ Being presented with a test when you are not ready for it
   ◆ Disrespect
   ◆ Girlfriend/boyfriend cheating
   ◆ Physical threat
   ◆ Gossip

3. Explain *perceived threat:*
   ◆ A perceived threat happens anytime we feel physically or emotionally threatened or at risk that something that we perceive as bad is about to happen to us.

◆ Perceived threat may be different for different people. How does that understanding help us to see that we have a choice in our reaction to a triggering event?

ACTIVITY: NEGATIVE AND POSITIVE SELF-TALK

With your co-facilitator, role-play two scenarios.

Scenario 1: Negative Self-Talk

Role-play one person (A) putting down another person (B). After being insulted, person B shares his or her negative self-talk. For example: "How dare you!" "He thinks he is all that!" "I'll show him," and "I'll get you later!"

Discuss the effect of self-talk on the anger reaction. Would the self-talk increase/escalate or decrease/deescalate the anger reaction?

Scenario 2: Positive Self-Talk

Role-play one person (A) putting down another person (B). After being insulted, person B shares his or her positive self-talk. For example: "She must be having a bad day," "I can handle this," and "It's not worth the price to fight."

NOTE: Do not confuse positive inner dialogue with positive thinking, happy affirmations, or self-delusions. Using logical, accurate self-talk means recognizing one's personal shortcomings, but it also helps put them in perspective and define a do-able plan of action. Positive self-talk (and smiling) activates three "happy messengers" in the brain: serotonin, noradrenaline, and dopamine. These brain chemicals begin to malfunction with negative self-talk.

Again, discuss the effect of self-talk on the anger reaction. Would the self-talk increase/escalate or decrease/deescalate the anger reaction?

---

4. If you wish, conduct the More Self-Talk Role Play and the Push/Push Back versus Push/Give activities, beginning on page 32.

5. Discuss:

◆ The *primary emotion* that is triggered by a putdown. *(hurt, betrayal, feeling disrespected and devalued, and so forth)*

◆ The resulting *anger reaction.*

It's easier to "do" anger than to express hurt, betrayal, fear, and the like.

We know how to "do" anger, and anger is more socially acceptable, especially for boys. Hurt, for example, is less socially acceptable.

◆ Hindsight: When we look back at a situation, it is often then that we see more clearly how our anger reaction actually cost us more than it was worth.

6. Discuss the importance of:

◆ Beginning to notice your anger elevate.

◆ Understanding the process of the anger reaction.

◆ Seeing and owning the negative outcomes your anger may cause.

7. Tell students:

◆ Remember when we say "So-and-so MAKES us angry," we give away our power. We become like a puppet on a string, and other people are pulling the strings. Do we want to be someone's puppet?

ACTIVITY: REACTING TO BLAME ROLE PLAY

Facilitators or two students role-play a short "blaming" scenario:

◆ Point to the other person and exclaim to everyone that he or she did X (pick a trigger), and it's his or her fault you are angry. The person MADE you angry. Ask the students, "Who has the power?" Most will immediately recognize that the other person has the power.

Now reverse the situation:

◆ Say instead that the person in the room "triggered your anger" when they did X. Then ask again, "Who has the power?" Most students will recognize the difference and answer that you have kept your power.

Summarize the points made and insights learned. Discuss as appropriate.

Closing thought: When we own our triggers and our anger, we keep our power.

Optional Activity: More Self-Talk Role Play

Use further role-play or discussion exemplifying how different self-talk will lead to a different primary emotion and, therefore, a different reaction. Role-play scenarios that might cause the following self-talk:

◆ Making "should" statements (or thoughts) about another person. These negative thoughts lead to a sense of injustice: "She should not act that way."

◆ Thinking about revenge and getting even: "I'd like to beat him down," "I want to kill him," "How dare she do that to me?" "He can't get away with that," or "I'll get her back."

◆ Assuming that the other person hurt you deliberately. This leads to thinking, "She did this on purpose."

◆ Taking things too personally: "She doesn't care about me."

◆ Making a big deal out of something another person might feel is small.

◆ Making judgments: "Wimps and weaklings need to be taught a lesson" or "He can't get away with acting like that."

◆ Negative self-talk: "It's not fair" or "He's mean."

Ask for a student volunteer to help you demonstrate the technique.

Step 1: Push/Push Back

◆ The facilitator and the student face each other at an arm's distance, both with the same foot forward.

◆ The forward hand of each participant is raised to approximately chest height, with the palm facing out, and the palm of the hand lightly touching the same part of the other person's hand.

◆ The rear hand (the hand corresponding to the rear foot) is placed gently on the elbow of the other person's lead elbow so that both players are in an equal starting position. (This also allows for a measure of safety, so neither the student nor facilitator gets pushed off balance.)

◆ Feet should be comfortably placed so that each person feels balanced and stable from the start.

◆ The facilitator then pushes, using an open palm, against the student's open palm until the student reacts. Most of the time, the student will instinctively push back. Typically, unless one party is much stronger than the other, there is a stalemate. Stop after a few seconds. DO NOT PUSH until someone falls or becomes endangered because of being off balance.

◆ Note the energy required to push, the thought processes, and any emotional reactions. Discuss what happened and why it happened.

If the student does not push back, go to Step 2, then redo the demonstration, directing the student to push back this time.

Step 2: Push/Give

◆ The facilitator and the student face each other at an arm's distance, both with the same foot forward.

◆ The forward hand of each person is raised to approximately chest height, with the palm facing out, and the palm of the hand lightly touching the same part of the other person's hand.

◆ The rear hand (the hand corresponding to the rear foot) is placed gently on the elbow of the other person's lead elbow so that both players are in an equal starting position. (This also allows for a measure of safety, so neither the student nor facilitator gets pushed off balance.)

◆ Feet should be comfortably placed so that each person feels balanced and stable from the start.

◆ The facilitator then instructs the student to push, using his or her open palm against the facilitator's open palm. Rather than push back, the facilitator gives in to the push and goes with it, stepping to the side (going to the side that the body naturally moves).

◆ Another option is for the facilitator to bend at the knees a bit and let the push go past him or her, staying grounded. This movement causes the pusher to lean too far forward and become off balance. In either reaction, the facilitator keeps his or her power by remaining in control and balanced.

◆ Discuss what happened and why it happened. Note the energy required to push, the thought process, and any emotional reaction.

Chemical Abuse and Emotions

The body is made up of billions of cells. Cells of the nervous system, called *neurons,* are specialized to carry messages through an electrochemical process.* The human brain has about 100 billion neurons.

Communication of information between neurons is accomplished by the movement of chemicals across a small gap called the *synapse.* Chemicals called *neurotransmitters* are released from one neuron at what is called the *presynaptic nerve terminal.* Neurotransmitters then cross the synapse, where they may be accepted by the next neuron at a specialized site called a *receptor.* Once attached, different neurotransmitters either trigger "go" signals that allow the message to be passed on to other cells or produce "stop" signals that prevent the message from being forwarded.

There are many different types of neurotransmitters, each of which has a precise role to play in the functioning of the brain. Generally, each neurotransmitter can bind only to a very specific matching receptor. Therefore, when a neurotransmitter couples with a receptor, it is like fitting a key into a lock.

These brain chemicals, or neurotransmitters, enable us to express our emotions (happiness, sadness, anger, and so forth). They give us the ability to learn, to be physically coordinated, and to store information in our memory or recall information when it is needed. The manufacture of

---

*The information provided for this lesson and the next has been derived from the sources listed at the end of this introduction.

neurotransmitters such as *serotonin, dopamine, adrenaline,* and *acetylcholine* is generated through complex biochemical pathways.

Insufficient or out-of-balance neurotransmitters can produce mood swings, anxiety, and depression. Sometimes the brain may have too many of one type of chemical or not enough of another. As a result, we may feel too high or too low, too sleepy or too alert.

The following definitions of neurotransmitters relate to chemical abuse and emotions and supplement the definitions and information presented in Lesson 3.

Dopamine is the main neurotransmitter in the brain. It causes increased mental alertness and awareness. Dopamine controls our moods, energy, and feelings of pleasure. When dopamine is prevented from release, or when there is too little of it in the brain, feelings of depression and/or discontent result.

Serotonin is the neurotransmitter responsible for the five senses, sleep, aggressive behavior, eating, and hunger. When released, it brings about feelings of calm, happiness, peace, and satisfaction. Sufficient amounts of circulating serotonin also signal feelings of fullness and reduce appetite. If the levels of serotonin are decreased or serotonin is blocked in the brain cells, aggression and violent behavior may result. Low levels of serotonin are linked with depression and increased appetite. Serotonin, in short, is a very powerful mood enhancer and appetite regulator.

Noradrenaline, also known as **norepinephrine,** has a stimulating effect on the brain. It gives the person a "pickup." It is most responsible for regulating the heart, breathing, body temperature, and blood pressure. It may also play a role in hallucinations and depression.

Adrenaline, also known as **epinephrine,** controls paranoia and the fight-or-flight response. It is also responsible for our appetite and feelings of thirst.

Of the three most important neurotransmitters—serotonin, noradrenaline, and acetylcholine—**acetylcholine** is the neurotransmitter used most when a person is under greater stress. Also responsible for muscle coordination, nerve cells, and memory, it is involved in the transmission of nerve impulses in the body.

Endorphins and **enkephalins:** Other brain chemicals (opioid peptides) that affect mood significantly are endorphins. Endorphins are very powerful natural opiates in the brain that produce feelings of intense pleasure. They can also reduce and relieve pain. You might have heard of the "runner's high." This has to do with the release of "feel-good" endorphins after a long run or exercise session. Endorphins also help us to handle stress. Enkephalins are other opiod peptides that, like endorphins, help the body to fight pain.

❧❧❧

Other brain chemicals control functions such as growth, allergies, and immune systems. A healthy brain contains a finely tuned balance of all the brain's neurotransmitters, or brain chemicals.

Addictive drugs activate the brain's pleasure circuit. Drug addiction is a biological, pathological process that alters the way in which the pleasure center, as well as other parts of the brain, functions. To understand this process, it is necessary to examine the effects of drugs on neurotransmission. Almost all drugs that change the way the brain works do so by affecting chemical neurotransmission. Some drugs, like heroin and LSD, mimic the effects of a natural neurotransmitter. Others, like PCP, block receptors and thereby prevent neuronal messages from getting through. Still others, like cocaine, interfere with the molecules that are responsible for transporting neurotransmitters back into the neurons that released them. Finally, some drugs, such as methamphetamine, act by causing neurotransmitters to be released in greater amounts than normal.

The following chart is for facilitator use as background information in this lesson. It is not intended to be presented to students. This level of detail is unnecessary for the purposes of the lesson and would likely overwhelm students.

Resources

Hanna, Nydia. (1990). *Drugs: The altered brain.* Center City: MN: Hazelden.

National Institute on Drug Abuse. (2005, November 25). *Mind over matter: Teaching guide* (NIDA for Teens). Retrieved June 2, 2006, from http://teens.drugabuse.gov/mom/tg_effects.asp

Drugs and Their Effects

Drug	Chemical it affects or replaces	Effect while on the drug	Effect after the drug is worn off
Alcohol	Alters serotonin levels. Substitutes for endorphins. Brain realizes that it doesn't need to make as many endorphins as it did before drinking alcohol became frequent. Therefore, it produces fewer endorphins.	Sleepiness or violent or aggressive behavior. Covers up depression. Dulls pain.	Sleep disturbance, depression, not enough endorphins present in the body to relieve normal, everyday pain. Craving for more alcohol to produce the chemical that substitutes for endorphins to reduce pain.
Anti-anxiety Drugs *For example, Valium, Xanax, Ativan, Centrax, Serax, Librium, Equanil, Librax, Paxipam*	Substitute for endorphins and enkephalins at anxiety receptor sites. Can drain the brain's natural stores of neurotransmitters in five weeks. Restoring the balance is a long process.	Produce a calm or comfortable mood.	Create a craving for the drug. Anxiety may return. Withdrawal can cause seizures and depression.

Stimulants

Amphetamines

Speed, crank, crystal, black beauties, white cross, uppers, dexies, bennies, meth (methamphetamine), and ice.

Many prescription amphetamines.

Cause excess release of dopamine, norepinephrine, epinephrine, serotonin, enkephalins, and glutamate. Once these chemicals are released, they are used up by the brain. They are not recycled into the brain cells. The brain can't produce enough neurotransmitters to replace those used, so it operates on a low level of neurotransmitters.

Mood heightened; user is excited, talkative, and confident.

Dry mouth, sweating, headache, blurred vision, dizziness, and anxiety. Long-term use may cause strange and frightening behavior. User may "crash" (experience severe depression) when the drug wears off.

Adapted from National Institute on Drug Abuse, *Mind over Matter: Teaching Guide* (NIDA for Teens), November 29, 2005. Retrieved June 2, 2006, from http://teens.drugabuse.gov/mom/tg_effects.asp

DRUG	CHEMICAL IT AFFECTS OR REPLACES	EFFECT WHILE ON THE DRUG	EFFECT AFTER THE DRUG IS WORN OFF
Stimulants (continued)			
Cocaine and Crack	Alter at least 10 neurotransmitters in the brain. Current research indicates that the effects may be long lasting. Release excess dopamine. Dopamine is not recycled in the brain. Instead, cocaine molecules block the gates where dopamine would reenter the cell for up to 72 hours. Some dopamine is lost. Each cocaine use releases less and less dopamine because there is less in the cells. Some chemical changes cocaine causes in the brain may take a year to correct after cocaine use is stopped.	Unequaled high, feelings of superhuman abilities, release from boredom Feelings of paranoia, overactivity, stuttering	Person "crashes," becoming severely depressed. Sudden personality change Changes in the sex hormones. In some users, desire for sex and the ability to perform are reduced. It may take weeks for them to return to normal after cocaine use is ended. Cocaine can damage the ability to feel pleasure. Research suggests that long-term cocaine use may reduce the amount of dopamine or the number of dopamine receptors in the brain.

Mixed-Action Drugs

Pain Medications *For example, morphine, codeine, heroin*	Take the place of endorphins and enkephalins at three pain receptors.	Change mood, alleviate pain	Craving for more of the drug to replace the lesser production of the natural pain relievers Not enough endorphins and enkephalins present in the body to relieve normal, everyday pain.
Prescription Drugs *For example, Demerol, Dilaudid, Talwin, methadone, Percodan, Darvon)*	Substitute for endorphins and enkephalins at the brain's pain receptors. The brain slows production of endorphins and enkephalins. Also affect dopamine, serotonin, and norepinephrine.		
Marijuana	Affects brain and reproductive organs. Affects nine neurotransmitters. Almost doubles the action of serotonin. Heavy users (5–8 joints per day) for five years may have memory lapses for up to a year after they stop using. All users lose memory and ability to concentrate.	Changes perception and causes mellow feeling of well-being. Causes memory lapses and difficulty in concentration, increased appetite, dryness of mouth, increased pulse rate, and delusions and hallucinations.	Causes an imbalance of the brain's chemicals and creates withdrawal symptoms of its own. Decreased appetite, insomnia, fatigue, irritability, mood swings and depression

Drug	Chemical it affects or replaces	Effect while on the drug	Effect after the drug is worn off
Mixed-Action Drugs (continued)			
Inhalants	Volatile hydrocarbon compounds stimulate the brain cells, causing them to raise the level of neurotransmitters greatly. Once the neurotransmitters are released, they are used up. They aren't recycled into the brain cells, and the brain can't make up what has been lost. This creates a low level of neurotransmitters in the brain cells.	Give users a powerful "rush."	Often cause a crash, or deep depression. Can cause severe and permanent damage to the brain and body.
Ecstasy (MDMA) Has both stimulant (amphetamine-like) and hallucinogenic (LSD-like) properties.	Harms neurons that release serotonin. Chemical makeup varies, so it is difficult to say exactly what is affected each time.	User can feel confused or anxious, experience distortion of sound and vision. May feel "up" and have loads of energy.	Causes brain damage and memory impairment. May cause insomnia, anxiety, irritability, and paranoia. Affects mood, impulse control, and sleep cycles. May trigger Parkinson's disease.

Chemical Abuse and Emotions

Key Concepts

◆ Drugs affect emotions and the ability to manage anger successfully.

◆ Students' awareness of the impact of drugs on their ability to manage anger is critical to their ability to make sound choices.

Materials

Chemical Abuse and Emotions (Chart 4.1)

Neuron, Synapse, and Receptors (Chart 4.2)

Flip chart *(blank pages as needed to diagram different drugs substituting for brain chemicals in different receptors)*

Procedure

1. Initiate an interactive dialogue about chemical abuse and its effects on emotions.

   NOTE: When working with most middle school students, it may be sufficient to minimize the drug discussion to the effects of marijuana and alcohol.

2. Ask students:

   ◆ Have you ever lost your temper when you were sick, overtired, or not well?

   ◆ Was it more difficult to contain your anger when you weren't feeling well?

   ◆ Is it easier to manage anger if you are feeling good, healthy, or content?

- How does how you feel before a triggering event affect how you deal with a situation?
- If you are depressed, stressed, or in pain, can you have the personal strength and presence of mind that you need to manage anger well?

Chemical Abuse and Emotions

1. Present Chart 4.1 to explain how drugs affect the brain and consequently a person's emotions, moods, and ability to manage anger.

   #### Chemical Abuse and Emotions

   Mood-altering drug upsets brain chemical balance.

   Brain adjusts by making *less* of the natural chemical.

   Brain *requires* drug to maintain balance.

2. Ask students:
   - Name one common drug or substance that you know is used among your age group or possibly among adults or friends with whom you associate. Do not give people's names. The goal here is to list a drug that, if used, might affect your life, relationships, or interactions.

Neuron, Synapse, and Receptors

1. Present Chart 4.2, a version of the following diagram without the shapes that indicate drug/chemical substitutes or blocked receptors.

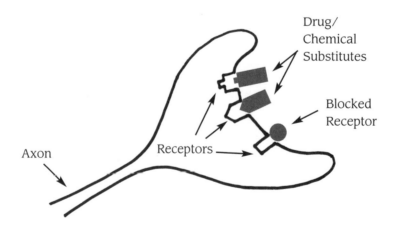

2. Diagram how the drugs that students name affect their emotional well-being during and after use. Examples for three drugs—marijuana, alcohol, and cocaine—are provided at the end of this lesson.

> *Closing thought: Managing anger and emotions requires being cool, calm, and centered, and drugs interfere with your ability to do this.*

EXAMPLE: MARIJUANA

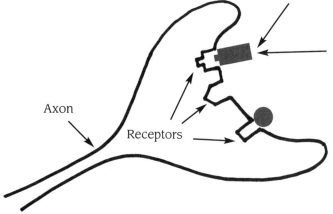

Use a different shape to represent different chemicals being replaced by drugs of use. See the table on pages 38–42 for descriptions of these chemicals and their effects.

Axon

Receptors

If students call out *marijuana,* you could say that pot replaces the natural receptor for serotonin, therefore causing an imbalance in the brain. The brain signals that it has too much serotonin and stops producing it. When the drug wears off, the brain does not have enough serotonin, which consequently causes withdrawal symptoms.

Serotonin affects sleep, mood, and memory. If the brain has an imbalance of serotonin because of marijuana use, there will be decreased appetite, insomnia, fatigue, irritability, mood swings, and depression.

Discuss the implications for anger management. Ask:

◆ If you feel these effects, will you be able to manage your anger well?

◆ If people you are dealing with feel these effects, how will they manage their anger?

Use a different shape to represent the different chemicals being replaced by drugs used. See the table on pages 38–42 for descriptions of these chemicals and their effects.

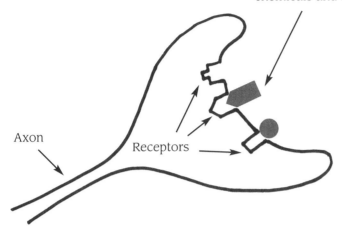

Axon

Receptors

If students call out *alcohol,* say that alcohol alters serotonin levels and substitutes for endorphins, therefore causing an imbalance in the brain. The brain signals that it has excess endorphins and slows down its natural production of them. When the alcohol wears off, the brain does not have endorphins.

Low post-drinking serotonin levels affect sleep. Also, there are not enough endorphines present in the body to relieve normal, everyday pain. (Afterwards, people get a hangover—and a hangover is painful.)

Discuss the implications for anger management. Ask:

◆ If you feel these effects, will you be able to manage your anger well?

◆ If people you are dealing with feel these effects, how will they manage their anger?

◆ Do you manage anger well if you are in physical pain?

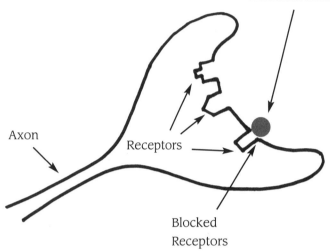

Use a different shape to represent different chemicals being replaced by drugs of use. See the table on pages 38–42 for descriptions of these chemicals and their effects.

Axon

Receptors

Blocked Receptors

If students call out *cocaine,* say that cocaine releases excess dopamine. Dopamine is not recycled in the brain (as it is supposed to be). Instead, cocaine molecules block the gates where dopamine would reenter the cell for up to 72 hours. Some of the dopamine is lost.

Cocaine can damage a person's ability to feel pleasure. When the drug wears off, users are often unable to feel pleasure, happiness, or other emotions. They often become severely depressed.

Discuss the implications for anger management. Ask:

◆ If you feel these effects, will you be able to manage your anger well?

◆ If people you are dealing with feel these effects, how will they manage their anger?

The Roles We Play

Key Concepts

◆ The "maps and pictures" in our heads and rules in our minds about how the world "should be" cause us to react to events with unconscious roles.

◆ Rather than making a conscious choice to act, we make unconscious choices to play the parts we need to play to survive according to our view of the world.

◆ Awareness of unconscious roles and rules is critical to managing our behavior and making conscious choices about how we manage our anger.

◆ The roles we play may not always allow us to make the choices that best serve our needs over the long term.

Materials

The Roles We Play (Chart 5.1)

Copies of the role-playing situations appropriate for your group (on pages 55–59)

Procedure

Conscious Roles

1. Present Chart 5.1.

    The Roles We Play

    Conscious roles

This lesson has been adapted by permission from *Why Is Everybody Always Picking on Me? A Special Curriculum for Young People to Help Them Cope with Bullying,* by Terrence Webster-Doyle, 1994, Middlebury, VT: Atrium Society Publications.

Unconscious roles

Why?

Consequences and effects

2. Ask students:

   ◆ What are some of the conscious roles that you play in life? For instance, when I'm here teaching this lesson, my conscious role is *(teacher, counselor)*. When I'm out with my *(mother, father, sister, brother)*, my conscious role is *(daughter, son, sister, brother)*.

   ◆ What is your conscious role here today?

   ◆ Do any of you have jobs at home or in the community?

   ◆ Do you volunteer?

   ◆ What type of jobs do you do?

   ◆ What is your role in these jobs? *(Often it is the job title.)*

   ◆ When you are with your friends, what is your conscious role?

   ◆ Do you act differently with your friends than on the job or when you are out with your family at a formal gathering? Why?

   ◆ Do you have different conscious roles when you are in different places or situations?

   ◆ Do those roles have learned rules of behavior?

   ◆ What is your role at school?

   NOTE: Once the students get the idea of what you are looking for, they freely come up with examples.

3. Ask students:

   ◆ How do our conscious roles affect our decisions about how we choose to act?

Unconscious Roles

1. Tell students:

   ◆ We also have unconscious roles that we take on when we are in different situations. They are unconscious roles because we don't realize that we "play" them.

◆ We are often unaware of when we fall into these roles; we don't realize how they influence our decisions and behavior, and we don't see the consequences of taking on these roles.

2. Ask the following questions and discuss student responses.

◆ How might a student act if the class is about to take a test and that student is not ready for the test or has no confidence that he or she will do well on the test?

◆ What unconscious role might that person play?

NOTE: It is important not to pass judgment here. The goal is to get students to see how they move into unconscious roles based on the rules they live by, their perception of the way things should be, or their need for protection against a threat. The difficulty with an unconscious role is that we react, rather than consciously act, and reacting often does not get us what we want for ourselves in the long term.

3. Ask students what unconscious roles might they play when. . . . *(Choose from the following situations to match your students' developmental age, circumstances, environment, and so forth.)*

◆ The teacher reprimands you in front of the class.

◆ A teacher/adult hovers over you when you are . . .

◆ You are out with your friends, and you don't have enough money to . . .

◆ You are with your boyfriend or girlfriend, and a stranger disses (disrespects) him or her.

◆ You are with your boyfriend/girlfriend, and your buddy disses him/her.

◆ Someone disses someone in your family.

◆ You are afraid of what your friends are going to think if you:

Don't fight.

Don't score. *(if age appropriate)*

Do well in school.

◆ If you *(don't fight, don't score, do well in school),* how might you act? What role might you take on?

◆ If you are afraid your date is not interested in sex, how might you act? *(This question may be appropriate for older teens because it is a very real source of anger stemming from gender-based "rules in our head.")*

4. Discuss:

- ◆ Why might someone take on the role of "macho man," victim, bully, and so on?

Why Do We Need to Understand the Roles We Play?

Tell students:

- ◆ If we can start to be aware of the roles we take on and understand why we do so, we can start to make conscious choices about how we want to live our lives.

- ◆ As long as we are reacting blindly, we may make choices that will seem "right" in the moment but be poor choices over the long term.

Consequences and Effects

Tell students:

- ◆ Poor choices often hurt others and are almost never in our own best interest.

  NOTE: Students may argue that "taking out" someone who wrongs them is right, good, or a "feel good" choice and, therefore, the best choice for them. Help them to think through the long-term consequences of their actions to see that poor choices may not help them to reach the goals they have set for themselves. In addition, poor choices do not necessarily guarantee that they will not be dissed, hurt, victimized, talked trash about, or otherwise wronged in the future.

ACTIVITY: HOW MIGHT I ACT? ROLE PLAY

Copy and cut out the role-play situations located at the end of this lesson. Choose the situations that are appropriate for your group. If possible, have students gather in a circle in chairs or on the floor.

- ◆ Put the role-play situations in a pile in the middle of the table or floor.

- ◆ Encourage students to take turns choosing a role and acting out their response. Students may read the situation aloud before they act it out, or they may choose a role of their own for other students to guess.

After each role play, discuss the following questions:

  What did you observe?

Have you seen similar behavior in your classrooms, at playgrounds, at home, or elsewhere?

How does the behavior help?

How does it hurt?

Is it a short-term win?

Is it a long-term win?

Does the behavior cause problems?

What else could someone choose to do instead?

Does the behavior cause anger?

Does the behavior avoid or reduce anger?

Closing thought: Be conscious of the "rules in your head" and the roles that you take on. Make choices that get you what you want in the long term instead of reacting quickly, in the moment.

Role-Play Situations for Middle and High School

The teacher passes out a test, and I'm afraid I'll fail. How might I act?

I have to do a presentation, and I'm scared of speaking in front of lots of people. How might I act?

The gym teacher insists that I play basketball, and I'm not good at sports. How might I act?

My gym class is doing a ropes course, and I'm scared I'll fall. How might I act?

I'm asked to help, and I'm afraid I'll make a mistake. How might I act?

Kids ask me about my grades, and I'm afraid they'll tease me about them. What might I say?

From *Transforming Anger to Personal Power: An Anger Management Curriculum for Grades 6–12,* by S. G. Fitzell, © 2007, Champaign, IL: Research Press (800–519–2707, www.researchpress.com)

I'm in a new group, and I'm afraid people won't like me. How might I act?

I'm afraid if I'm nice, kids will think I'm a wimp. How might I act?

Kids ask me to go places with them, but I'm shy with people I don't know. How might I act? What might I say?

When I'm in a group, I worry that I'll have nothing to say. How might I act?

When I'm with my friends, I think I talk too much. How might I act?

I want to do well, but I'm scared I'm not good at anything. How might I act?

My parents are huge sports fans, and I'm afraid I'll lose in the playoffs. How might I act?

If I'm friends with someone the other kids think is a loser, I'm afraid they will think I'm a loser, too. How might I act?

I'm afraid I'll look stupid if I wear my new shirt. How might I act?

I'm afraid my parents won't love me anymore if I don't pass my classes. How might I act?

Role-Play Situations for High School Only

I worry about what my friends are going to think about me if I don't score. How might I act?

I worry about what my friends are going to think about me if I don't fight. How might I act?

I worry about what my friends are going to think about me if I get good grades. How might I act?

I'm afraid that my date is not interested in sex. How might I act?

I'm afraid that my date might pressure me to have sex. How might I act?

From *Transforming Anger to Personal Power: An Anger Management Curriculum for Grades 6–12,* by S. G. Fitzell, © 2007, Champaign, IL: Research Press (800–519–2707, www.researchpress.com)

Emotions and Self-Talk: Perceptions

Key Concepts

This lesson pulls together the previous lessons into the following concepts:

◆ People perceive and interpret the same situation differently, have different self-talk and, therefore, different emotional responses.

◆ Self-talk directly affects how we feel.

Materials

For this activity, cover the words ANGRY and ANNOYED and their corresponding faces on the MOODZ chart.

Copies of MOODZ (Chart 6.1) to distribute to students as a handout

Copies of the Emotions, Self-Talk, and Perception Answer Sheets *(for middle school or high school, as appropriate for your group)*

Procedure

1. Give each student a copy of Chart 6.1. Explain that students will be using this chart in the lesson.

Anxious	Guilty	Sad
Bored	Happy	Satisfied
Cautious	Hopeful	Shy
Confused	Hysterical	Silly
Depressed	Lonely	Smitten
Disgusted	Nasty	Surprised
Distrustful	Nervous	Thrilled
Embarrassed	Overwhelmed	
Frustrated	Really Tired	

Emotions and Self-Talk

2. Tell students:

◆ The exercise we will do today will help us to pull together what we've learned so far. For the process to work, it is very important to have some ground rules.

◆ I am going to ask you to react to a situation. Please do NOT comment out loud. It is important that you don't influence one another by your reactions to certain scenarios. Please respect the process so that everyone can get what he or she needs out of today's lesson.

◆ This is one of the few times that you will be asked to write. Draw your response if you like, but it needs to go on paper so that you remember it when we discuss the results. Another reason for writing the answers is to keep your response private.

◆ After I have read all the scenarios, I will ask you to share your answers. If you are uncomfortable sharing what you wrote, you have the right to pass. Just say, "I pass."

◆ Use the feelings poster to help you decide what people might be feeling. You may not use the word *angry* or any words that mean *angry.* You may only use primary emotion words.

ACTIVITY: REFLECTION SCENARIOS

◆ Distribute the answer sheet appropriate to your age group, then read the corresponding situations from the Emotions, Self-Talk, and Perception Scenarios lists, beginning on page 65.

◆ Allow enough time for students to fill out their answer sheets.

Usually, at least one student in the group will choose not to fill out the answer sheet. Often students who do not write out the answers still participate appropriately in the discussion afterwards.

◆ Encourage, but do not force, students to respond in writing. Some students simply cannot. It is best not to make an issue of a refusal to write.

◆ Do a round-robin for each scenario to hear the different reactions from students.

◆ Point out how different students react very differently:

Different students use different feelings words.

Self-talk varies from person to person.

Positive self-talk feeds positive or neutral actions.

◆ Draw conclusions from the group. What did they learn from this exercise?

Closing thought: Our self-talk (you think it) triggers our emotions (you feel it) and prompts our reactions (you do it.) You think it, you feel it, and you do it! Adjust your thinking so that you make choices in YOUR best long-term interest.

Emotions, Self-Talk, and Perception: Middle School Scenarios

1. Mike walks into a movie theatre and sees a group of teens he knows from school. When he walks over to join them, one of the guys whispers, just loud enough for Mike to hear, "Oh, no. Here comes Mike, the fag."

    a. How might you feel if you were Mike?

    b. What self-talk comes to mind?

2. Maria and Carlos have been going out together for about two months. Carlos knows about Maria's old boyfriend, Rick. One day Maria and Carlos are in the cafeteria having lunch when Rick walks in and asks if he can sit with them.

    a. How might you feel if you were Carlos?

    b. What self-talk comes to mind?

3. Jim and his younger bother, Gil, are playing a strategy game. Their father walks in and sees Jim make a bad move. He looks at Jim with disgust and asks, "Why don't you THINK before you make such a stupid move?"

    a. How might you feel if you were Jim?

    b. What self-talk comes to mind?

4. An unfamiliar group of teen boys is hanging out on the street corner. Elaina walks by, and one of the boys whistles and calls her over while the others laugh and start to move towards her.

    a. How might Elaina feel?

    b. What self-talk comes to mind?

5. Fred's older sister, Lucy, is constantly making fun of him at home and at school. He was passing Lucy and her friends on the way home from school when Lucy mockingly called out, "Hey you, loser! I can smell you from here!"

    a. How might Fred feel?

    b. What self-talk comes to mind?

6. Rachael and Siobhan were on opposite sides of the cafeteria. Rachael came up to Siobhan and said, "Melinda said you were talking trash about her with Jo. She's really mad at you." Siobhan knew she had not talked about Melinda.

    a. How might Siobhan feel?

    b. What self-talk comes to mind?

Emotions, Self-Talk, and Perception: High School Scenarios

1. Mike walks into a movie theater and sees a group of teens he knows from school. When he walks over to join them, one of the guys whispers, just loud enough for Mike to hear, "Oh, no. Here comes Mike, the fag."

    a. How might you feel if you were Mike?

    b. What self-talk comes to mind?

2. Maria and Carlos have been going steady for about two months. Carlos knows about Maria's old boyfriend, Rick. One day Carlos and Maria are at the local hangout having coffee and donuts when Rick walks in and asks if he can join them.

    a. How might you feel if you were Carlos?

    b. What self-talk comes to mind?

3. Jim and his younger bother, Gil, are playing a strategy game. Their father walks in and sees Jim make a bad move. He looks at Jim with disgust and asks, "Why don't you THINK before you make such a stupid move?"

    a. How might you feel if you were Jim?

    b. What self-talk comes to mind?

4. An unfamiliar group of teen boys is hanging out on the street corner. Elaina walks by, and one of the boys whistles and calls her over while the others laugh and start to move towards her.

    a. How might Elaina feel?

    b. What self-talk comes to mind?

5. George and Erica have been going steady for months. George sees the star football player, Blake, talking to Erica after games and in the hall at school. When George confronts Erica about it, she denies there's a

problem and says, "If you have a problem, why don't you do something about it?"

    a. How might George feel?

    b. What self-talk comes to mind?

6. Rachael and Siobhan were on opposite sides of the cafeteria. Rachael came up to Siobhan and said, "Melinda said you were talking trash about her with Jo. She's really mad at you." Siobhan knew she had not talked about Melinda.

    a. How might Siobhan feel?

    b. What self-talk comes to mind?

Emotions, Self-Talk, and Perception

Mike's emotion	Mike's self-talk
Carlos's emotion	Carlos's self-talk
Jim's emotion	Jim's self-talk
Elaina's emotion	Elaina's self-talk
Fred's emotion	Fred's self-talk
Siobhan's emotion	Siobhan's self-talk

From *Transforming Anger to Personal Power: An Anger Management Curriculum for Grades 6–12,* by S. G. Fitzell, © 2007, Champaign, IL: Research Press (800–519–2707, www.researchpress.com)

Emotions, Self-Talk, and Perception

Mike's emotion	Mike's self-talk
Carlos's emotion	Carlos's self-talk
Jim's emotion	Jim's self-talk
Elaina's emotion	Elaina's self-talk
George's emotion	George's self-talk
Siobhan's emotion	Siobhan's self-talk

From *Transforming Anger to Personal Power: An Anger Management Curriculum for Grades 6–12,* by S. G. Fitzell, © 2007, Champaign, IL: Research Press (800–519–2707, www.researchpress.com)

Expressing Feelings

Key Concepts

◆ Ways that we choose to express our anger can either escalate or deescalate anger in others or ourselves.

◆ There are four basic ways that people deal with anger.

◆ How people express anger is a learned behavior.

◆ How we express our feelings, including anger, is a choice we make.

◆ How we express our emotions has consequences.

Materials

Ways to Express Anger (Chart 7.1)

Expressing Anger (Chart 7.2)

Copies of the Four Ways to Express My Anger handout (on page 75)

Blank flip-chart pages *(to list ways of dealing with anger)*

Procedure

Ways People Express Anger

Present Chart 7.1.

Ways to Express Anger

Escalates ⇑   Deescalates ⇓

ACTIVITY: BRAINSTORM AND EVALUATE

Ask students:

◆ How do people express their anger?

◆ How do they deal with it?

If necessary, lead with a scenario of how someone might deal with anger. For example, someone calls you a name, and you respond by punching her, or someone calls you a name, and you laugh and walk away.

List on a flip chart:

◆ Ways students say people deal with anger. (Fill one or two blank flip-chart pages.)

◆ Do not place a value judgment on the methods.

Define:

Escalate: Increase in extent or intensity. (Makes the situation worse.)

Deescalate: Reduce the level or intensity. (Makes the situation better.)

Ask:

◆ How might these methods escalate or deescalate the conflict triggering the anger?

Review:

◆ Consider each method for expressing anger listed on the flip chart.

◆ In front of each method, draw an up arrow or a down arrow to indicate whether the method might escalate or deescalate a conflict. Some items will have both up and down arrows.

Discuss:

◆ Why the methods might escalate or deescalate anger and the circumstances that might cause either result.

◆ Remember to consider the person towards whom the anger is being expressed when deciding whether the method escalates or deescalates the conflict.

Four Ways to Express My Anger

1. Give students a copy of and review the Four Ways to Express My Anger handout.*

---

*This handout has been adapted by permission from material in *Change Is the Third Path: A Workbook for Ending Abusive and Violent Behavior,* by M. Lindsey, R.W. McBride, and C.M. Platt, 1993, Littleton, CO: Gylantic Publishing Company.

2. Ask:

- ◆ When might it be appropriate to use each of the four ways to express anger?

- ◆ Are there some ways that are never appropriate or helpful?

- ◆ If our goal is to find ways to express our emotion or anger so that we keep our power and help ourselves in the long term, which ways might be better choices?

3. If time allows, conduct the optional role play described on page 74.

Expressing Anger Is Difficult

1. Present Chart 7.2.

   Expressing Anger

   Why is it difficult to deal with anger?

   How do we learn to deal with anger?

   Who are our role models?

   How does our self-talk influence how we express anger?

2. Ask and discuss the questions listed on the chart.

   Closing thought: We can choose to express our anger in ways that help us to keep our power and support our future goals, or we can choose to express anger in a way that gives away our power and undermines our ability to have the future we want. What will we choose for ourselves?

OPTIONAL ACTIVITY: EXPRESSING ANGER ROLE PLAY

Use role-playing to enact the four ways to express anger:

◆ I can stuff it.

◆ I can escalate it.

◆ I can handle it directly.

◆ I can handle it indirectly.

Students may write a script for their role play ahead of time or act out a scenario spontaneously.

Discuss body language; facial expression; visible escalation, if present; and other issues that arise.

NOTE: Role-playing can start to feel quite real if the "actors" get into their parts. Take care to monitor emotions and behaviors so real conflict does not result from the activity.

Four Ways to Express My Anger

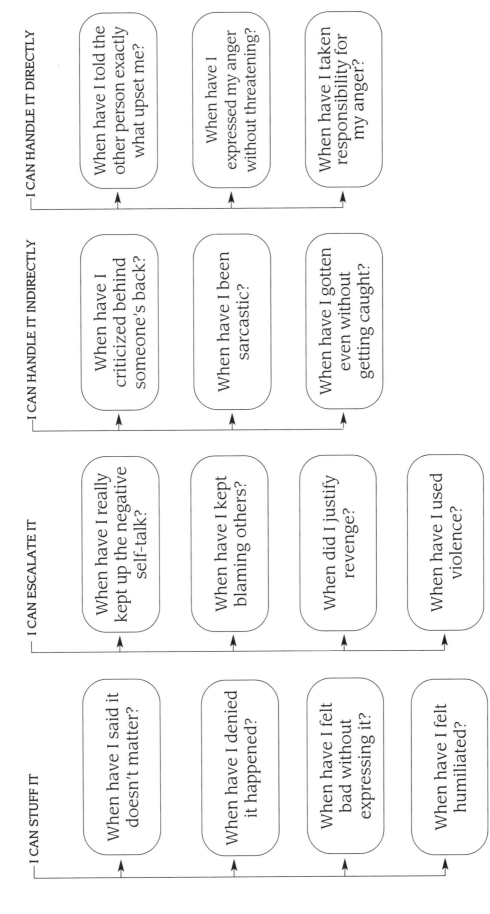

I CAN STUFF IT

- When have I said it doesn't matter?
- When have I denied it happened?
- When have I felt bad without expressing it?
- When have I felt humiliated?

I CAN ESCALATE IT

- When have I really kept up the negative self-talk?
- When have I kept blaming others?
- When did I justify revenge?
- When have I used violence?

I CAN HANDLE IT INDIRECTLY

- When have I criticized behind someone's back?
- When have I been sarcastic?
- When have I gotten even without getting caught?

I CAN HANDLE IT DIRECTLY

- When have I told the other person exactly what upset me?
- When have I expressed my anger without threatening?
- When have I taken responsibility for my anger?

From *Transforming Anger to Personal Power: An Anger Management Curriculum for Grades 6–12,* by S. G. Fitzell, © 2007, Champaign, IL: Research Press (800–519–2707, www.researchpress.com)

Keeping Your Power

Key Concepts

◆ Depending on how we react to a conflict or perceived threat, we either give up our power or keep our power.

◆ We have options for keeping our power.

◆ We can identify and practice healthy choices for dealing with emotions, conflict, and anger.

Materials

You've Got the Power (Chart 8.1)

Keeping Your Power (Chart 8.2)

Fight or Flight: Not the Only Route to Survival (Chart 8.3)

More Healthy Choices (Chart 8.4)

Copies of the "I" Statements, Stopping Conflict in Its Tracks, and Thought Stopping handouts

Procedure

You've Got the Power

1. Present Chart 8.1.

   You've Got the Power

   How do we give up our power?

   Through blame: If we choose to believe that someone else is responsible for our feelings, we are giving away our power.

   Through expectations: Because of someone else's action or inaction, we choose to feel . . .

   When we feel we can change someone else.

2. Discuss:

◆ What is one way we can give up our power? *(blame)*

◆ If we choose to believe that someone else is responsible for our feelings, we are giving away our power.

◆ We are saying, in essence, "I can't control myself, so you are controlling me. I have no power to control myself."

◆ If I blame you, I am saying that you are responsible for my anger, and therefore I cannot be responsible for myself. If I am not responsible for myself, I have no power. I give my power away to you.

◆ If I own my behavior and take responsibility for myself, you cannot make me feel anything I do not want to feel. You cannot hurt me. You cannot control me because I am in control of and responsible for myself. I have my power. You can't have it.

ACTIVITY: REVERSING BLAME

A technique that helps us understand the other person's point of view and avoid blame is to ask ourselves why we are wrong.

◆ Choose a scenario in which blame is assigned.

◆ Ask students to come up with as many reasons as they can to justify the behavior of the person being blamed.

NOTE: Often, if we can honestly complete this exercise when we are tempted to cast blame, it becomes more difficult to blame the other person. Our anger lessens or is replaced by calm.

---

3. Discuss:

◆ What is the second way we give up our power? *(expectations)*

◆ I control my expectations. When I expect something from you and you do not meet my expectations, who is responsible for my anger?

◆ My expectations are my choice. If I set expectations for another person and become angry when the person doesn't meet them, I give away my power over my emotions to that person. The person can control my emotions simply by not meeting my expectations.

4. Discuss:

   ◆ What is a third way we can give up our power? *(when we feel we can change someone else)*

   ◆ If I base my happiness on whether someone will change, then I give that person the power over my emotions. When my self-talk is "I wouldn't get angry if he'd change," then whether another person changes or not becomes the trigger for my emotions (anger). The other person is in control. The other person can control my emotions simply by changing or not changing.

5. Discuss:

   ◆ How these statements can be applied to students' lives, personal situations, and conflicts. Try to get students to see how the three ways of giving away power apply to them personally.

Keeping Your Power

1. Present Chart 8.2.

   Keeping Your Power

   Be aware when anger is surfacing.

   STOP and think!

   Self-talk: Positive or negative?

   Strategies

   Stay in control.

   Keep your cool.

   Make a healthy choice.

2. Tell students:

   ◆ You have a choice. You do not need to be a puppet on a string (or a fish on a hook), reacting to another person's moves.

   ◆ You have the choice to keep your power or to give it away.

   ◆ You can choose to be powerful in a way that brings you POSITIVE consequences.

   ◆ When you are taunted, rather than blame, make a positive choice for yourself. You do not have to be someone's puppet (or take the bait and bite on a bully's hook).

3. Discuss the points on the chart, one at a time.

Be aware when anger is surfacing.

◆ Many of us are conditioned to ignore anger signals. We start to escalate our anger, and we don't even notice until we are furious and possibly out of control.

◆ Remember "fight or flight" from the second lesson? Can we notice when we are starting to get angry? What are the signals in our bodies?

STOP and think!

◆ Once you notice your body signals, be a thought detective. What is your self-talk? Is it positive or negative?

Use strategies.

◆ Stay in control! You've caught your body reactions and thoughts; now you can choose to use your skills.

◆ Keep your cool! When you lose your cool, you give away your power.

◆ Make a healthy choice.

Fight or Flight: Not the Only Route to Survival

1. Present Chart 8.3.

   Fight or Flight: Not the Only Route to Survival

   Throw a curve: Do the unexpected.

   Use positive self-talk.

   Stand in the other person's shoes.

   Be assertive.

   Keep it light.

   Ask yourself: Is it worth the price I will pay if I fight?

2. Discuss each of the strategies.

Throw a curve—do the unexpected.

◆ When someone is triggering our anger, either deliberately or unintentionally, one of the best strategies for managing the situation is to do something unexpected.

◆ If the person is deliberately taunting you, that person thinks he or she can take your power and expects you to react in a negative way. Trick the person by doing the unexpected:

Smile and nod.

Agree with part of what the person is saying, thank the person, and walk away.

Pretend it's a compliment.

Stay very calm and cool, and respond with a "caring" question. For example, "Why does that bother you?"

NOTE: These strategies and more are listed in the Stopping Conflict in Its Tracks handout on page 88.

Use positive self-talk.

◆ I can handle this!

◆ This isn't my problem. I'm OK.

◆ Fighting isn't worth the price.

Stand in the other person's shoes.

◆ Often students will say "stupid people" make them angry. They sometimes find it difficult to define what they mean by "stupid people." If we can try to understand why people act "stupid," we are more likely to be able to manage our response.

◆ Empathy is necessary to understand the motives of annoying people. When we realize that people act "stupid" because they might be hurt, anxious, under stress, and so forth, it helps us to lessen our anger response.

Be assertive.

◆ Use "I" statements to express how you feel and what you need.

Keep it light

◆ Use humor to deal with tense situations.

◆ Be careful to avoid sarcasm and put-downs.

Ask yourself, "Is it worth the price I will pay if I fight?"

◆ What is the price (consequence) of fighting? Is it worth it in the long term?

NOTE: Young people have a difficult time considering the long term. They need us to help them see that the win today may be the loss tomorrow and the next day and the next day, and so on.

3. If you wish, have students do the optional role-play activity described on page 85.

NOTE: Additional strategies are listed in the Stopping Conflict in Its Tracks handout.

More Healthy Choices

1. Present Chart 8.4.

More Healthy Choices

Assert with "I" statements.

Walk away (with head held high).

Stop a conflict in its tracks.

Call "time out."

Empathize.

Thought stop.

Defend without violence.

2. Conduct the following activities.

ACTIVITY: ASSERT WITH "I" STATEMENTS

Give students a copy of and review the "I" Statements handout (page 86).

◆ As a group, develop a conflict scenario.

◆ Brainstorm a script, including assertive actions to address the conflict scenario.

◆ Have two students role-play.

   Student 1 plays the instigator of the conflict.

   Student 2 uses the script.

◆ Instruct the onlookers to watch body language and tone of voice.

Discuss student observations, emotions experienced, and insights gained.

ACTIVITY: WALK AWAY WITH HEAD HELD HIGH OR CALL A TIME OUT

Discuss the idea that walking away with strength means making a conscious choice to use walking away as a strategy for keeping your power.

◆ Have two students role-play.

Student 1 attempts to instigate a fight.

Student 2 walks away with head held high.

◆ Student 2 acts out the following instructions:

Take one step back and one step to the side.

Put both hands in front of your torso, waist high and close to your body. Do *not* reach into the other person's space.

In a very strong voice, say, "I refuse to fight," "Don't touch me!" "Time out," "We can discuss this when we calm down," or something similar.

Walk away without turning your back to the instigator, with shoulders back and head held high! (Put a book on the student's head if necessary to teach this important component of body language.)

ACTIVITY: STOPPING CONFLICT IN ITS TRACKS

Give students a copy of and review the Stopping Conflict in Its Tracks handout (on page 88).

◆ Discuss the types of conflict we find ourselves in when we allow ourselves to be sucked into bantering, arguing, or fighting with someone.

◆ Brainstorm ways to use the phrases on the Stopping Conflict in Its Tracks handout. (Adapt the phrases on the handout to reflect current adolescent slang.)

◆ Role-play conversations, using the suggested phrases and words from the handout in response to another person's verbal attack, teasing, criticism, accusations, and so on.

OUTSIDE ACTIVITY: THOUGHT STOPPING

Give students a copy of and review the Thought Stopping handout (on page 90).

◆ Tell students that thought stopping can help students to control the obsessive, negative self-talk that often fuels anger.

◆ Ask:

Between now and our next meeting, see if you can catch yourself feeding negative self-talk. When you catch negative self-talk taking over, try a thought-stopping technique and see what works for you. If one technique doesn't help, try a different one. The purpose here is to find one more way to keep your power.

OPTIONAL ACTIVITY: THROWING A CURVE ROLE PLAYS

Ideally, these role plays will be spontaneous. You may use ready-made scripts; however, the activity works best if students make them up on the spot, using situations that are real to them with language that is typical in their environment.

◆ Two students role-play:

> Student 1 plays the instigator, deliberately attempting to trigger the other's anger.

> Student 2 uses anger management skills.

◆ The student being taunted may choose to respond with one of the following strategies:

> Smile and nod.

> Agree with part of what the person is saying, say thank you, and walk away.

> Pretend it's a compliment.

> Stay very calm and cool and respond with a "caring" question. For example, "Why does that bother you?"

Other role-play options can be found in the Stopping Conflict in Its Tracks handout.

"I" Statements

"I" statements can take many forms. As you get comfortable using them, you will most likely find a variety of ways to phrase them. When learning, it is helpful to start with a formula.

First

Think about who owns the problem (Whose problem is it?) If you are upset, it's *your* problem. If another person is upset, it's *that person's* problem. If you care about the relationship, it's *our* problem.

Second

Think about how you'd express your feelings, using the following template:

1. I feel _____ *(angry, hurt, scared . . .)*
2. When _____ *(say what happened)*
3. Because _____ *(why it upsets you)*
4. And I would like _____ *(what you want to happen or change)*

For example:

"When you interrupted me, I felt angry because I was feeling disrespected," instead of "You make me furious when you keep interrupting me!"

The second statement not only blames the other person, it also gives away your power.

Take the statement up another level by adding, "I would appreciate it if you didn't interrupt me when I'm speaking."

From *Transforming Anger to Personal Power: An Anger Management Curriculum for Grades 6–12,* by S. G. Fitzell, © 2007, Champaign, IL: Research Press (800–519–2707, www.researchpress.com)

(page 1 of 2)

CAUTION

◆ Be careful that the "I" statement is not really a disguised "you" statement. Avoid using the words *that* or *like* in your statements. These words muddy up what you are trying to communicate and are often loaded with judgment or negativity. For example, "I feel that you . . ." or "I feel like you . . ." really attack the listener. The phrase "I feel" should always be followed by an emotion word.

◆ Try to avoid using words for *anger* in your "I" statements. Anger emotion words often cause the other person to stop listening. Try to use primary emotion words to express how you feel, even if that means that you step away in the moment and take some time to reflect on what the emotion underlying the anger is. It's easier for the listener to hear "I feel overwhelmed . . .," "I feel disrespected . . .," or "I feel hurt . . ." than it is to hear "I feel angry . . . (or other slang and more inflammatory words for the anger emotion)."

"You" statement that escalates conflict	*"I" statement for the same issue*
"You don't care about me!"	"I feel neglected when you ignore me."
"You hit on my girlfriend/ boyfriend!"	"I feel disrespected when you flirt with . . ."
"You are an inconsiderate jerk!"	"I feel betrayed when you criticize me."

Stopping Conflict in Its Tracks

When you find yourself caught in a verbal exchange that does not feel right, then you may be dealing with bullying—intimidation, bulldozing, sarcasm, pushiness, exploitation, manipulation, and so forth.

You may also simply be dealing with someone who is upset over a misunderstanding and unable to communicate clearly in the moment.

First

Recognize and pay attention to your body signals: Don't ignore discomfort, an adrenaline rush, or other physical signs.

Second

Stop, breathe, and think: "I can handle this" (use positive self-talk).

Third

◆ Act consciously (as opposed to reacting).

◆ Be conscious of your body language and the words you choose: KEEP YOUR POWER.

Use verbal responses that don't escalate conflict:

◆ "I see."

◆ "Thank you for letting me know how you feel."

◆ "I hear you."

◆ "Ouch!" (Cues the other person that he/she is being hurtful. Sometimes the person doesn't realize it.)

◆ "I can see this upsets you."

◆ "I'm sorry you were hurt. That was not my intent."

From *Transforming Anger to Personal Power: An Anger Management Curriculum for Grades 6–12,* by S. G. Fitzell, © 2007, Champaign, IL: Research Press (800–519–2707, www.researchpress.com)

◆ "I shouldn't have to defend myself, and I won't."

◆ "Excuse me, I'm not finished." *(Say softly.)*

◆ "Agree with *some* of the statement, but not all." (For example, "You have a chip on your shoulder because you're short." Agree: "Yes, I am short.")

◆ "You have an interesting perspective."

◆ "I'll have to give that some thought."

◆ "I'll talk to you when you're calm." (Call "time out" and leave.)

◆ "I'll talk to you when I'm calm." (Call "time out" and leave.)

◆ "Thanks for the compliment."

Ask a question: The person who asks a question keeps the power.

◆ "Why does that bother you?"

◆ "How so?"

◆ "Why do you ask?"

◆ "What makes you say that?"

◆ "I know you wouldn't have said that unless you had a good reason. Could you tell me what that is?"

Tips for success

◆ Stay calm.

◆ Be careful about tone of voice.

◆ Lower your voice.

◆ Avoid "should," "ought," and "would" statements.

Thought Stopping

Thought stopping can help you control the obsessive, negative self-talk that often fuels anger. Follow these steps to stop negative thoughts:

Step 1

Become aware that you are obsessing on negative self-talk. For example, you are thinking about the person you are angry with and going over the situation in your head, repeatedly. Often, your self-talk gets more violent and more intense in the process.

Step 2

Stop and think about what you are doing. Be a thought detective.

Step 3

Deliberately do something that will distract your mind from the negative self-talk. For example:

◆ Shout, "Stop!" or "Stop! I'm keeping my power!" Eventually, you might be able to simply whisper, "Stop," and your mind will be free of the angry self-talk.

◆ Visualize a bright red stop sign.

◆ Put an elastic band around your wrist and, when you catch yourself obsessing over the situation, snap the elastic so you feel a slight sting.

◆ Pinch yourself lightly on the arm and visualize a bright red stop sign.

Step 4

Substitute these thoughts for the obsessive thoughts:

◆ "I can handle this!"

◆ "My time and energy is worth more than this!"

◆ "It's not worth it."

From *Transforming Anger to Personal Power: An Anger Management Curriculum for Grades 6–12*, by S. G. Fitzell, © 2007, Champaign, IL: Research Press (800–519–2707, www.researchpress.com)

Program Conclusion

*Ideally, the program conclusion takes place in a separate meeting.
If this is not possible, it can be presented as part of Lesson 8.*

Key Concepts

◆ We have a choice to defend ourselves without violence.

◆ We have strategies that allow us to keep our power and stick up for ourselves.

Materials

Copies of the Techniques That Preserve Your Power handout

Procedure

1. Discuss:

   ◆ How we defend ourselves without violence.

2. Ask:

   ◆ What have we learned in these sessions?

   ◆ What one strategy will you take with you and use often?

   ◆ What technique will help you keep your power by managing your anger?

3. Give students the Techniques That Preserve Your Power handout and discuss.

4. If possible, keep the door open to participants in the future because they will need reinforcement and support. What students have learned in the many years they have lived cannot be unlearned in eight lessons. You have planted seeds and given them tools. They are on their way to practicing skills to manage their anger. It's only the beginning for them.

Techniques That Preserve Your Power

What Can You Do Instead of Fighting?

◆ Throw a curve—do the unexpected.

◆ Stay centered.

◆ Use positive self-talk.

◆ Stand in the other person's shoes, or empathize.

◆ Be assertive.

◆ Keep it light.

◆ Smile and nod, smile and nod.

◆ Ask yourself, "Is it worth the price I'll pay if I fight?"

Keep Your Power

◆ Be aware when anger is surfacing

◆ STOP and think!

◆ Ask yourself, "Is my self-talk positive or negative?"

Use Your Strategies

◆ Stay in control

◆ Keep your cool.

◆ Make a healthy choice.

The Person Who Asks the Question Is in Charge

◆ I guess that's your opinion, but why do you want to tell me that?

◆ Why are you bringing it up to me?

◆ What's wrong with . . . ?

◆ What do you think?

◆ Can you tell me more?

◆ What do you mean?

◆ Is that bad? Good?

Phrases That Stop Conflict in Its Tracks

◆ I see . . . That's an interesting perspective.

◆ I'll give that some thought.

◆ You may be right.

◆ It must be hard for you. *(Empathize)*

◆ I can see you're angry right now, let's . . .

From *Transforming Anger to Personal Power: An Anger Management Curriculum for Grades 6–12,* by S. G. Fitzell, © 2007, Champaign, IL: Research Press (800–519–2707, www.researchpress.com)

APPENDIX A
Sample Charts

Anger Management:
An Opportunity

◆ Ground rules

◆ Why are you here?

◆ You have a choice: Open mind or closed mind.

◆ Expectations

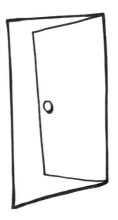

Unlock the door of opportunity!

From *Transforming Anger to Personal Power: An Anger Management Curriculum for Grades 6–12,* by S. G. Fitzell, © 2007, Champaign, IL: Research Press (800–519–2707, www.researchpress.com)

Are the Following Statements True?

◆ _I have the right_ to feel what I feel.

◆ My feelings are valid.

◆ I am fully _responsible_ for my feelings; I own what I feel.

From _Transforming Anger to Personal Power: An Anger Management Curriculum for Grades 6–12,_ by S. G. Fitzell, © 2007, Champaign, IL: Research Press (800–519–2707, www.researchpress.com)

Name Some Primary Emotions

ANGER is a secondary emotion.

2.3

We Own Our Feelings

◆ Responsibility = Ownership

◆ No one can put feelings inside of us.

◆ No one can _MAKE_ us angry.

◆ People _TRIGGER_ our anger.

◆ We _CHOOSE_ how we feel.

We Have a Choice

◆ Accept your feelings

<u>AND</u>

◆ Choose your actions wisely.

Are you a puppet on a string?

When We Feel Angry . . .

◆ We are not **BAD** . . . we are angry.

◆ What we do with that anger is a choice we make.

◆ If we make a mistake, we are not bad . . . we are learning.

Physiological Definitions

▶ Noradrenaline: Neurotransmitter regulates

▶ Adrenaline

▶ Stimulus/stimuli = trigger

How does your body feel when you get _ANGRY?_

What Makes You Angry?

Triggers Your Anger?
What ~~Makes You Angry?~~

Anger Reaction!

- ◆ Triggering event
- ◆ Perceived threat
- ◆ Physical reaction
- ◆ Negative self-talk
- ◆ Primary emotion
- ◆ **<u>ANGER REACTION</u>**
- ◆ Hindsight

Chemical Abuse and Emotions

◆ Mood-altering drug upsets brain chemical balance.

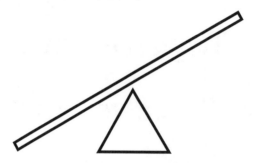

◆ Brain adjusts by making *less* of the natural chemical.

◆ Brain *requires* drug to maintain balance.

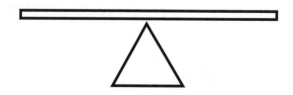

Neuron, Synapse, and Receptors

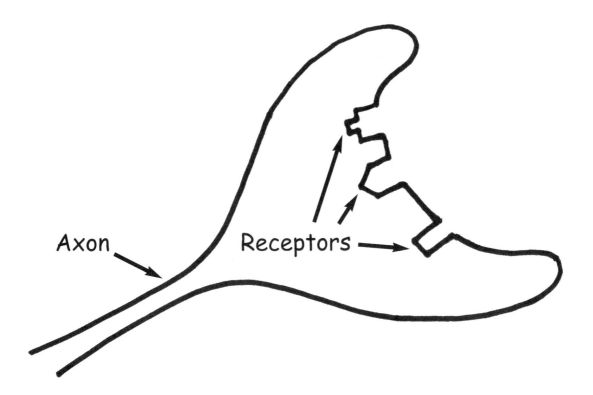

The Roles We Play

◆ Conscious roles

◆ Unconscious roles

◆ Why?

◆ Consequences and effects

From *Transforming Anger to Personal Power: An Anger Management Curriculum for Grades 6–12,*
by S. G. Fitzell, © 2007, Champaign, IL: Research Press (800–519–2707, www.researchpress.com).
Illustrations © 2006 by Shivan Fitzell. Reprinted by permission.

Ways to Express Anger

Escalates ⬆   **Deescalates** ⬇

From *Transforming Anger to Personal Power: An Anger Management Curriculum for Grades 6–12,* by S. G. Fitzell, © 2007, Champaign, IL: Research Press (800–519–2707, www.researchpress.com)

Expressing Anger

◆ Why is it difficult to deal with anger?

◆ How do we learn to deal with anger?

◆ Who are our role models?

◆ How does our self-talk influence how we express anger?

You've Got the Power

How do we give up our power?

◆ _Through blame_

If we choose to believe that someone else is responsible for our feelings, we are giving away our power.

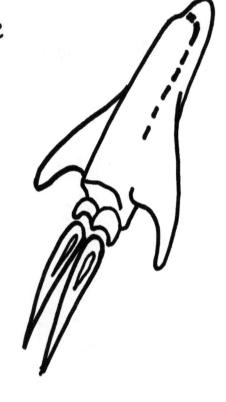

◆ _Through expectations_

Because of someone else's action or inaction, we choose to feel . . .

◆ <u>_When we feel we can change someone else._</u>

From _Transforming Anger to Personal Power: An Anger Management Curriculum for Grades 6–12,_ by S. G. Fitzell, © 2007, Champaign, IL: Research Press (800–519–2707, www.researchpress.com)

Keeping Your Power

◆ Be aware when anger is surfacing.

◆ **STOP** and think!

    Self-talk:
Positive
or negative?

◆ Strategies

    Stay in control.

    Keep your cool.

    Make a healthy choice.

From *Transforming Anger to Personal Power: An Anger Management Curriculum for Grades 6–12,* by S. G. Fitzell, © 2007, Champaign, IL: Research Press (800–519–2707, www.researchpress.com)

Fight or Flight: Not the Only Route to Survival

◆ Throw a curve: Do the unexpected.

◆ Use positive self-talk.

◆ Stand in the other person's shoes.

◆ Be assertive.

◆ Keep it light.

◆ Ask yourself: Is it worth the price I will pay if I fight?

More Healthy Choices

◆ Assert with "I" statements.

◆ Walk away (with head held high).

◆ Stop a conflict in its tracks.

◆ Call "time out."

◆ Empathize.

◆ Thought stop.

◆ Defend without violence.

APPENDIX B
Anger Management Pretest and Posttest

The pretest and posttest included here satisfy the requirement for data collection. However, I do not believe a pretest or posttest can effectively evaluate the success of this program. A review of other researchers' attempts to evaluate the efficacy of anger management programs finds that most evaluations are fraught with challenges. These challenges include inconsistent and incomplete discipline referrals, difficulty measuring the real-time impact of the program when effects may not be manifested immediately, and the subjectivity of discipline policies in classrooms and schools. In addition, self-assessments, such as those included here, may not reflect growth as observed by adults.

Unless one can evaluate progress in the real-time experiences of the participants outside the group and compare that to behavior over a significant length of time, it is difficult to prove that a program works. However, students, their teachers, and data collected from office discipline referrals all attest to the fact that learning has happened and students have gained from the experience.

Anger Management Pretest

Name or ID _____ Date _____

True or False?

1. I have the right to feel what I feel.   T / F

2. My feelings are valid.   T / F

3. I own my feelings.   T / F

4. I can explain how I feel without using the word   T / F
   angry or a word that means angry.

5. People can make me angry.   T / F

6. If I get angry because of someone's stupid actions,   T / F
   it is his or her fault.

7. I cannot help it if I get angry.   T / F

8. I do not notice it when I start to get mad.   T / F
   It happens too fast.

9. Using drugs has no effect on managing anger.   T / F

10. Some drugs may affect moods even after   T / F
    they have worn off.

11. I am always aware of why I act the way that I do.   T / F

12. I am always aware of the rules that I live by.   T / F

Provide Short Answers

1. Write an example of a primary emotion.

2. Write an example of a secondary emotion.

From *Transforming Anger to Personal Power: An Anger Management Curriculum for Grades 6–12,*
by S. G. Fitzell, © 2007, Champaign, IL: Research Press (800–519–2707, www.researchpress.com)

3. Can your anger be controlled?

4. What is the fight-or-flight reaction?

5. List some things that you can do to deal with anger.

On a scale of 1 (Low) to 10 (High), rate the following about yourself:

1. I think that I will benefit from this program.
   Very little   1   2   3   4   5   6   7   8   9   10   **A lot**

2. How often do I become angry in a week?
   Never   1   2   3   4   5   6   7   8   9   10   **Often**

3. How often do I get in trouble because of my anger in a week?
   Never   1   2   3   4   5   6   7   8   9   10   **A lot**

4. I think I have good skills to deal with my anger
   No skills   1   2   3   4   5   6   7   8   9   10   **Many skills**

Anger Management Posttest

Name or ID _____ Date _____

True or False?

1. I have the right to feel what I feel.   T / F

2. My feelings are valid.   T / F

3. I own my feelings.   T / F

4. I can explain how I feel without using the word   T / F
   angry or a word that means angry.

5. People can make me angry.   T / F

6. If I get angry because of someone's stupid actions,   T / F
   it is his or her fault.

7. I cannot help it if I get angry.   T / F

8. I do not notice it when I start to get mad.   T / F
   It happens too fast.

9. Using drugs has no effect on managing anger.   T / F

10. Some drugs may affect moods even after   T / F
    they have worn off.

11. I am always aware of why I act the way that I do.   T / F

12. I am always aware of the rules that I live by.   T / F

Provide Short Answers

1. Write an example of a primary emotion.

2. Write an example of a secondary emotion.

From *Transforming Anger to Personal Power: An Anger Management Curriculum for Grades 6–12,*
by S. G. Fitzell, © 2007, Champaign, IL: Research Press (800–519–2707, www.researchpress.com)

(page 1 of 2)   **121**

3. Can your anger be controlled?

4. What is the fight-or-flight reaction?

5. List some things that you can do to deal with anger.

On a scale of 1 (Low) to 10 (High), rate the following about yourself:

1. I think that I benefited from this program.
    Very little   1   2   3   4   5   6   7   8   9   10   **A lot**

2. How often do I become angry in a week?
    Never   1   2   3   4   5   6   7   8   9   10   **A lot**

3. How often do I get in trouble because of my anger in a week?
    Never   1   2   3   4   5   6   7   8   9   10   **Often**

4. I think I have good skills to deal with my anger
    No skills   1   2   3   4   5   6   7   8   9   10   **Many skills**

Recommended Resources

The Atrium Society®
PO Box 816
Middlebury, VT 05753
Phone: (800) 848–6021
http://www.atriumsoc.org/

Change Is the Third Path: A Workbook for Ending Abusive and Violent Behavior, by Robert McBride, Michael Lindsay, and Constance Platt, 1996, Littleton, CO: Gylantic Publishing Company. *(Most recent edition of the book on which the handout "Four Ways to Express" anger is based.)*
Phone: (303) 773–2616
http://www.gylantic.com/change.htm

National Institute on Drug Abuse (NIDA)
National Institutes of Health
6001 Executive Boulevard, Room 5213
Bethesda, MD 20892–9561
Phone: (301) 443–1124
http://www.nida.nih.gov/drugpages.html

Simon's Hook: A Story about Teases and Put-downs, 1999, by Karen Gedig Burnett (Author) and Laurie Barrows (Illustrator). Roseville, CA: GR Publishing.

Phone: (831) 335–5366
http://www.grandmarose.com/

Talk, Trust & Feel Therapeutics
1120 Buchanan Avenue
Charleston, IL 61902
Phone: (217) 345–2982
http://members.aol.com/AngriesOut/

Violence Prevention Curriculum for Adolescents (Teenage Health Teaching
Module; Video and Teacher's Guide), by Deborah Prothrow-Stith, 1987,
Newton, MA: Education Development Center, Inc.
Phone: (617) 969–7100
https://secure.edc.org/publications/prodview.asp?656

A Volcano in My Tummy: Helping Children to Handle Anger, by Elaine
Whitehouse and Warwick Pudney, 1996, Gabriola Island, BC V0R 1X0
(Canada): New Society.
Phone: (250) 247–9737
http://www.newsociety.com/bookid/3733

For the world's longest list of feeling words: http://eqi.org/fw.htm

About the Author

SUSAN GINGRAS FITZELL, M.Ed., has been touching lives in public schools and beyond since 1980. She has over two decades of experience meeting the needs of youth with special needs and those who are coping with behavioral and anger management issues and bullying. She has co-facilitated anger management support groups for teens at the high school and middle school level since 1999. Susan's work focuses on building caring, inclusive school communities and helping students and teachers succeed in the inclusive classroom. Her other books include *Special Needs in the General Classroom: Strategies That Make It Work* (Cogent Catalyst); *Please Help Me with My Homework! Strategies for Parents and Caregivers* (Cogent Catalyst); and *Free the Children: Conflict Education for Strong, Peaceful Minds* (New Society).

A dynamic, nationally recognized presenter and educational consultant, Susan provides practical strategies to increase the achievement of all students in all classrooms. She is available for inservice training, keynote presentations, and consultation. For more information, contact:

Susan Gingras Fitzell
AIMH Educational Programs
PO Box 6182
Manchester, NH 03108
Phone: (603) 625-6087
http://www.aimhieducational.com/

NOTES